SEPTEMBER

Ellen Jackson

Illustrated by
Pat DeWitt and Robin DeWitt

![Charlesbridge] **Charlesbridge**

To Megan Schlueter—E. J.

To a wonderful husband and special
brother-in-law, Christopher John Grush
—P. D. & R. D.

Did You Know?

September is a month of traveling. Tiny seeds parachute into the wind, and burs hitch rides on socks and sweaters. In the Northern Hemisphere, many birds, fish, and butterflies travel south for the winter.

In the northern half of the United States, nights are cool, and the first frost glitters in the grass. Leaves show hints of copper or gold. When the wind gives them a tug, a few flutter to the ground. The September thorn, a tree often found in parks and along city streets, bears bright red fruit in the fall.

Animals get ready for the cold season in September. Harvester ants are hard at work collecting seeds and grain. Mice and chipmunks hide nuts and seeds to eat later when food is hard to find. A chipmunk can carry nine large nuts at a time—four in each of its cheek pouches and one between its teeth.

People, too, are busy preparing for the winter. Farmers work long hours in the fields harvesting grain and potatoes. Cotton is gathered in the South. In California, grapes are plump, purple, and ready to be picked. The farmers hope that September will be a mild month so that the crops will not be damaged. An old English rhyme begs the winds of September not to blow too hard: "September blow soft, / 'Til the fruit's in the loft."

Vacationers from the city board up their summer
cabins, and swimming pools close. Children crunch
leaves underfoot as they walk to school carrying
backpacks and wearing brand-new shoes. The first
day of school is exciting. It is time to start the next
grade and meet a new teacher. September also
brings high-school marching bands and the smell
of roasted peanuts at football games.

Many sports seasons begin in September. Soccer is the world's most popular team sport. People all over the world play some version of soccer, a game that can be played in parks, in empty lots, or on playgrounds. No special equipment is needed. Just grab a ball and have fun!

The weather is cool in September and just right for a game of tennis. Tennis is a sport enjoyed by people of all ages. Many United States presidents have played the game, including Theodore Roosevelt, Woodrow Wilson, John F. Kennedy, and Gerald Ford.

The September Birthstone

The birthstone for September is the sapphire. Many sapphires are blue, but they can also be blue-green, violet, yellow, or pink. People throughout history have thought that sapphires have magical powers. The ancient Greeks believed that these gems belonged to the god Apollo and could help foretell the future. In the Middle Ages, sapphires were thought to protect people against snakes.

The September Flower

If you were born in September, your special flower is the aster. *Aster* means "star" in Latin, and during September, these flowers are as common as stars. An ancient Greek myth tells how the goddess Asterea looked down upon the earth and wept because she saw no stars there. As her tears struck the ground, they turned into asters.

The September Zodiac

Virgo, the virgin, is the astrological sign for those people with birthdays from August 23 to September 22. People born under Virgo are said to be good at organizing things. They are also good at taking care of people and animals. A Virgo can be trusted with important tasks and responsibilities. But at times, a Virgo can be critical of others.

The sign for people born from September 23 to October 23 is Libra, the scales. Those born under Libra can see both sides of an argument, and they sometimes find it hard to make decisions. They are charming and polite. A Libra likes to be around people and often has many friends.

The Calendar

September is the ninth month of the year and has thirty days. In ancient Rome, the year began in March, not January. September was then the seventh month of the year. Its name comes from the Latin word *septem*, which means "seven."

Roman leaders wanted September to be named for a person, not a number. At various times, it was named for different Roman emperors. But none of these names was popular, and the month remained *September*.

A legend says that the rulers of ancient Rome changed the number of days in September back and forth. Finally Emperor Augustus gave it thirty days once and for all. In 1582, the calendar was adjusted once again by Pope Gregory XIII and September was made the ninth month of the year.

Sun, Sky, and Weather

Mist rises over fields and ponds on September mornings. The meadows still smell of hay and cut grass. On frosty mornings, you can see your breath in the cold air, but September afternoons are often sunny and warm.

The sun is lower in the sky than it was in August, and the evenings are cooler. At night, the Big Dipper hangs low in the northern sky.

Hurricanes usually appear in the Gulf of Mexico, the Caribbean Sea, and the Atlantic Ocean in late August and September. Sometimes they move onto land. These violent tropical storms bring heavy rains and winds that blow at least seventy-four miles an hour. Hurricanes can pull trees out of the ground and blow buildings apart. Heavy seas pound the coast and flood the roads.

The Anglo-Saxons, who settled in Britain in the fifth and sixth centuries, called September *Gerst monath*, or barley month, because it was the time when barley was ripe and ready to be made into a special drink. The September full moon has been called the harvest moon by some Native American peoples of the Northeast because farmers can harvest their crops by its bright light.

Animals in September

Woolly bear caterpillars look for cracks in the bark of trees for protection against the coming cold. These caterpillars are black and fuzzy with an orange-brown band in the middle. Some people believe that the winter will be harsh and severe if this band is thinner than usual and mild if the band is thick.

Ladybugs can sometimes be seen clustering together for warmth and protection near stream banks or under leaves on the forest floor. Each ladybug has an unpleasant odor. It is thought that when thousands cluster together, their strong smell repels predators.

Birds, such as tree swallows, robins, and ruby-throated hummingbirds, fly south in the fall looking for warmer weather and a place where they can find food more easily. In the spring, they will fly north again. The movement of animals from one place to another with the change of seasons is called migration.

Many male birds take on darker colors in the fall to help them hide from hungry enemies. Male goldfinches change from gold to olive, and male scarlet tanagers go from bright red to dull green. Other animals change their colors, too. Weasels, snowshoe hares, and caribou exchange their brown coats for snowy white ones in the fall.

Many reptiles and amphibians look for places to spend the winter. Wood frogs and spotted salamanders seek shelter under leaves or logs. Snakes look for holes or crevices between rocks. Hundreds of snakes sometimes winter together in one tangled pile.

Many mammals are fattening themselves up for the winter. Skunks grow plump on insects, frogs, snakes, fruit, and berries. Raccoons look for food in the woods or, if food is scarce, in city garbage cans and bird feeders. Bears gain a pound or more a day between August and October.

In the desert, wood rats gather food for the winter and arrange their nests. These animals eat mesquite leaves, desert grasses, and cactus pulp. They build mounds of earth, rocks, bark, tin cans, and bottle caps, and line the inside of the nests with soft grass.

Chimney swifts migrate to South America in the fall. In the city, these birds can be seen flying into chimneys, where they will roost for the night before continuing their journey. Inside the chimneys, the swifts cluster together, clinging to the walls with their claws.

Plants in September

Clusters of poisonous purple berries droop from the pokeweed plant. Ferns that were once green and lush are now dry and brown. Bouncing bet and joe-pye weed bloom in the woods. According to a legend, joe-pye weed was named for a Native American who cured illnesses with medicine made from this plant.

Hickory trees are heavy with nuts, and the leaves of sugar maples have begun to turn red. Falling September leaves form a thick carpet on the forest floor and provide a dark, moist place for mushrooms to grow.

Many plants and trees produce seeds in September. Jewelweed shoots its seeds into the air with a snap. The seeds of maples, ashes, and elms have little wings that help them float on the wind. It is fun to catch and toss the twirling maple seeds, which look like tiny helicopters. Many of these seeds will provide food for birds and mice, but others will stay hidden under the leaves until spring.

Although September is harvest time in most of North America, it is a time of new growth in the desert. Seeds have already sprouted after the summer thunderstorms. Desert grasses have sprung up, and shrubs and trees have put out new leaves. Tomatillo shrubs are dotted with little red fruit, and creosote bushes have a fresh, tangy smell.

In September, the last flowers of the season bloom on the prairie. Most of these are small plants tucked in among the tall grass, such as prairie gentians and ladies' tresses.

Special Days

Labor Day

Labor Day is a national holiday in the United States that is set aside to honor working people. Labor Day always falls on the first Monday in September. In the nineteenth century, labor unions wanted better and safer working conditions for people who worked long hours for little pay. Members of the Central Labor Union organized the first Labor Day parade and picnic in New York City on September 5, 1882. In 1884, that union urged groups in other cities to celebrate Labor Day. In the following years, some other states recognized the holiday. The United States Congress passed a law making Labor Day an official national holiday in 1894. Today many schools begin classes on the day following Labor Day.

The Equinox

You may have noticed that in the summer, the sun does not set until late in the evening. In the winter, the opposite is true. Night drops from the sky like an inky curtain in the late afternoon.

But on two days each year, the autumn and spring equinoxes, day and night are of equal length. The autumn equinox occurs around September 22. The word *equinox* comes from a Latin word that means "time of equal night."

September 22 is usually the first day of autumn in the Northern Hemisphere, which begins to cool as it receives less and less direct sunlight. Winter is on its way.

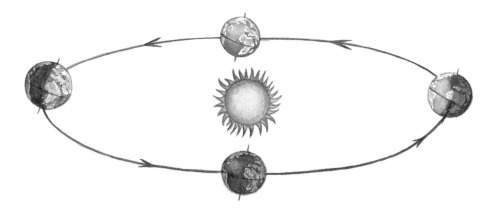

Rosh Hashanah and Yom Kippur

Two of the most important Jewish holidays occur in the fall around the time of the autumn equinox—Rosh Hashanah, the Jewish new year, and Yom Kippur, the Day of Atonement.

On the eve of Rosh Hashanah, Jews say special prayers and light candles. The next day, everyone goes to the synagogue. A ram's horn, called a shofar, is blown to announce the beginning of this special period. On Yom Kippur, ten

days later, many Jews fast to express their regret for any unworthy behavior. At sundown, the shofar is blown again, and the fast is over.

Famous September Events

On September 16, 1620, the *Mayflower* sailed
from Plymouth, England, carrying 102 Pilgrims
and crew members to the New World. The ship
was headed for the territory of Northern Virginia
near the Hudson River, where the Pilgrims
intended to settle. Because of some mistakes in
navigation, the *Mayflower* reached the coast of
present-day Massachusetts instead. There the
Pilgrims founded Plimoth Colony, which was the
first permanent settlement in New England. The
first European child born in New England, a boy
named Peregrine White, was delivered
on the *Mayflower* after
the ship had already
dropped anchor.

On September 23, 1846, Johann Gottfried Galle and Heinrich Ludwig d'Arrest observed an unknown planet for the first time. The planet was named Neptune after the Roman sea god. Neptune is the eighth planet from the sun and has eight moons.

On September 2, 1945, World War II ended when the Japanese surrendered to the Allies aboard the USS *Missouri* in Tokyo Bay. World War II was one of the most brutal wars in recorded history. Over fifty million people were killed, and countless others were injured.

Birthdays

Many famous people were born in September.

Seiji Ozawa

September 1, 1935

Music director of the Boston Symphony Orchestra and winner of Japan's Inouye Sho Award for lifetime achievement in the arts.

Gloria Estefan

September 1, 1957

Singer and musician, known as the Queen of Latin Pop.

Christa McAuliffe

September 2, 1948

Schoolteacher and first private citizen to fly on a space shuttle. She was killed when *Challenger* exploded on January 28, 1986.

Jane Addams

September 6, 1860

American worker for peace and the rights of women and co-winner of the Nobel Peace Prize in 1931.

Queen Elizabeth I

September 7, 1533

Queen of England from 1558 to 1603. Under her reign, England became a world power.

Jesse Owens

September 12, 1913

Track-and-field athlete and winner of four Olympic gold medals in the 1936 games.

Walter Reed

September 13, 1851

Army doctor known for his research on yellow fever.

Tommy Lasorda

September 22, 1927

Former manager of the Los Angeles Dodgers baseball team.

Mary Church Terrell

September 23, 1863

Women's rights activist, lecturer, and president of the National Association of Colored Women.

John Chapman

September 26, 1774

Better known as Johnny Appleseed. Frontiersman who planted apple trees throughout Ohio, Indiana, and Illinois.

A September Myth

The ancient Greeks believed that Zeus was the mightiest of the gods. When Zeus was a baby, he was cared for by nymphs who lived on the island of Crete. The nymphs had a fairy goat whose magical horns provided them with nectar and ambrosia, the food of the gods. Zeus, too, ate the magical food and grew into a strong, handsome god. After some time, he left the cave and eventually overthrew his father—an act that made Zeus ruler of the gods.

Years passed, and one day the goat died. The nymphs wept and could not be comforted. What could they eat now that the magical goat was dead? Zeus heard their cries and came down from Mt. Olympus.

"I want to thank you for all that you have done for me," he said, plucking one of the horns from the goat's carcass.

"This is your horn of plenty," he said. "It will always be full of flowers, fruits, and berries, and you will never lack for anything that Mother Earth can provide."

Then the nymphs saw that it was true. To this day, the horn of plenty, or the cornucopia, is a symbol of the autumn harvest and the wonderful gifts that come from the earth.

AUTHOR'S NOTE

This book gives an overview of the month of September in North America. But nature does not follow a strict schedule. The mating and migration of animals, the blooming of plants, and other natural events vary from year to year, or occur earlier or later in different places.

The zodiac sections of this book are included just for fun as part of the folklore of the month and should not be taken as accurate descriptions of any real people.

Many ancient people had myths and legends about autumn. The September myth is adapted from *D'Aulaires' Book of Greek Myths* by Ingri and Edgar Parin d'Aulaire. (New York: Bantam Doubleday Dell Publishing Group, 1962.)

Text copyright © 2002 by Ellen Jackson
Illustrations copyright © 2002
  by Pat DeWitt and Robin DeWitt
All rights reserved, including the right of
  reproduction in whole or in part in any form.

Published by Charlesbridge Publishing
85 Main Street, Watertown, MA 02472
(617) 926-0329
www.charlesbridge.com

Illustrations done in watercolor on Arches
  hot-press paper
Display type and text type set in Giovanni
Color separations made by Sung In Printing,
  South Korea
Printed and bound by Sung In Printing,
  South Korea
Production supervision by Brian G. Walker
Designed by Diane M. Earley

Library of Congress
Cataloging-in-Publication Data

Jackson, Ellen B., 1943-
    September/Ellen Jackson; illustrated by
  Pat DeWitt and Robin DeWitt.
      p.cm.—(It happens in the month of)
    ISBN 0-88106-922-1 (hardcover)
    1. September—Folklore. 2. September—
  Juvenile literature. [1. September.] I. DeWitt,
  Pat, ill. II. DeWitt, Robin, ill. III. Title.

GR930.J345   2002
398'.33—dc21   2001023512

Printed in South Korea
10 9 8 7 6 5 4 3 2 1